LOW-KEY

AND HATER-FREE

A STATEMENT. A MISSION. A LIFESTYLE.

CHARLES E TYLER

FOREWORD

Let me take you back for a second. Over 20 years ago, I met a friend who would go on to leave a lasting impact on my life. He's one of the coolest people I've ever known—a rare gem. The kind of guy whose wisdom sticks with you long after the conversation ends. We've had a lot of deep talks over the years—some serious, some funny, most of them in the most ordinary of settings. But one day, he dropped a phrase that hit different.

I asked him how he was doing, and in his usual, cool but subtle way, he said:

"Low-key and hater-free."

He said it casually, just like he always does. No big speech, no explanation—just dropped it in the middle of the conversation like it was nothing. But for some reason, that one phrase stuck with me. It rhymed, sure, but it also resonated with me on a deeper level. I started thinking about it: What does it mean to be *low-key*? What does it look like to live *hater-free*?

I began repeating it, sitting with it, really breaking it down in my own mind. The more I thought about it, the more I realized this wasn't just a cool saying—it was a *life philosophy*. One that shows up in how we carry ourselves, how we navigate the world, and how we protect our peace.

To me, being low-key and hater-free is about humility, intentionality, authenticity, and peace of mind. It's about staying grounded and true to yourself, even when the world around you is loud, flashy, and full of distractions.

Now that I'm a proud son, father, grandfather, uncle, nephew, cousin, friend, and coworker, I find myself reflecting on how I've lived and the lessons I've learned along the way. These aren't just lessons for me;

they're ones I want to share with whoever finds them and help them live a life of purpose, peace, and authenticity.

As a young man, I loved being involved, taking charge, and contributing in any way I could. My mother would've killed me if I didn't. I watched her do things in the community and follow her passion for history. She set a powerful example of being present and engaged. It was always about stepping up, leading, and engaging in something meaningful. No matter how high I would climb, I didn't want to lose that grounded mindset. And hearing that phrase from my friend reminded me of something I've always believed: you don't have to be loud to be powerful. You don't need to seek attention to have value.

I also think of my father, who passed away but was a very loving and low-key man. He didn't seek attention, but he loved people and lived an effortless, quiet life. Both of my parents instilled in me that helping people, loving people, and doing good things aren't about the awards or recognition. It's about doing it with purpose, being genuine, and staying true to who you are—no matter your socioeconomic status or whether anyone knows what you're doing. It's about being authentic, being you, and never letting your environment or the things you possess control who you are or what you stand for.

In today's world—where everything is hyper-connected, and everyone's got an opinion I think we need this reminder more than ever.

But before we dive in, I want to make one thing clear:

This isn't a book about hiding or being antisocial. It's not about playing small or disconnecting from life.

Being low-key doesn't mean being invisible; it means moving with purpose, not pressure.

It means protecting your peace. It means not giving access to people who don't deserve a front-row seat in your life.

It's not about doing less—it's about doing what *matters*. And being hater-free? It's not about pretending everything's perfect. It's about choosing not to be consumed by other people's negativity. You can still lead, love, and live out loud—but you do it your way. With grace, wisdom, and energy protected.

Whether you're looking to find peace, level up your mindset, or create some space from all the noise, this book is your guide.

I hope it challenges you to take a deeper look at your habits, relationships, and the way you move through the world. It's a reminder that success doesn't always need a spotlight—and that peace is a power all its own.

Stay low. Stay cool. Stay grounded.

Let's go.

Table of Contents

CHAPTER ONE:

THE POWER OF STAYING LOW-KEY AND HATER-FREE

Introduction: What It Means to Be Low-Key and Hater-Free

We live in a world where everything's happening *now*. Everyone's sharing everything—their wins, their struggles, their thoughts, their meals—24/7. With so many voices clamoring for attention, it's easy to get caught up in trying to stand out. I'm not immune to it; in fact, I've been there myself. Growing up, I was always told to be loud, to stand out, to fight for my spot in the world. But here's the thing: there's an art to moving in silence, to working behind the scenes without broadcasting every single step. That's what it means to stay low-key.

Being low-key doesn't mean being invisible or lacking ambition. Quite the opposite. Being low-key is about confidence—confidence in yourself and your purpose without the need for outside validation. It's about having the self-assurance to work quietly, to grow steadily, and to let your results speak for themselves. You value privacy and purpose over popularity, and when you're low-key, you're focused on what matters most to you.

Being hater-free is just as important. In a world full of opinions, judgment, and negativity, it's crucial to protect your peace. Haters will always exist. But when you learn how to rise above the noise, you protect your energy and focus on what matters—your journey, your purpose, and your success.

Why Low-Key and Hater-Free Are Essential Today

In a world that's always moving, it's easy to get lost in the chaos. But living low-key and hater-free can help you navigate the world with a sense of peace, purpose, and clarity. Here's why:

✓ *You Protect Your Energy:*

When you keep your plans, dreams, and goals to yourself, you shield them from unnecessary negativity and doubt. Not everyone deserves a front-row seat to your journey. The less you reveal, the less room there is for outside criticism or distractions to seep in.

✓ *You Move Smarter, Not Harder:*

The less you reveal about your plans, the more freedom you have to adapt and grow without interference. When no one knows your every move, they can't interfere or distract you. This gives you the ability to work in your own flow and stay focused.

✓ *You Let Success Speak for Itself:*

There's something powerful about accomplishing your goals quietly. When you finally achieve what you set out to do, the results speak louder than any announcement or boastful post could. Success is undeniable when it's earned with quiet consistency.

✓ *You Avoid External Pressure:*

The more people know about your plans, the more opinions you invite. Staying low-key reduces external pressure and noise, letting you focus solely on your goals and the work it takes to achieve them.

✓ *You Discover Who Really Supports You:*

Staying low-key helps you see who truly cares about you and your success. People who are genuinely in your corner will support you whether you're posting about it or not. Those who only show up when it's convenient will disappear when things get tough.

My Journey to Staying Low-Key

For much of my life, I wanted to be seen and heard. I worked hard to prove myself, to show the world what I could do. But over time, I realized that being loud wasn't necessary to be impactful. I learned the value of moving in silence of building without boasting—and of staying grounded no matter how high I climbed.

One of my biggest moments of growth came during a tough career transition. I didn't post about it. I didn't explain myself to anyone. I focused inward, set my goals, and did the work behind closed doors. When I finally emerged on the other side—better, stronger, and more successful—it was a reminder that the results always speak louder than the process.

A New Street Saying: Glow Up in the Shadows

Here's something to live by: *Glow up in the shadows.* It means you don't need the spotlight to shine. Work on yourself, improve your skills, and let your results do the talking when the time comes. Don't rush the process—let the growth happen naturally and without noise.

In fact, we need a new phrase here. Instead of "keeping up with the Joneses," let's call it *"rising with the currents"*—it's about moving with intention, without the need for constant validation or comparison.

Action Steps to Start Living Low-Key

Ready to embrace the low-key lifestyle? Here are a few actionable steps to get started:

✓ **Start a private journal:** Write down your goals, dreams, and progress without sharing them publicly. This is your personal space for reflection and growth.

✓ **Share less on social media:** Not every win or milestone needs to be posted. Share what feels authentic, and keep the rest for yourself.

✓ *Limit your circle:* Confide in a small group of trusted friends or mentors who genuinely have your best interests at heart. Quality over quantity.

✓ *Work consistently:* Stay focused on your goals, even when no one is watching. Success comes with time and effort—not noise and attention.

✓ *Celebrate quietly:* Learn to appreciate your progress without needing external validation. The internal satisfaction is worth so much more.

The power of staying low-key lies in its simplicity. You're not running away from success; you're building it quietly, one step at a time. By the time people notice, your results will already speak for themselves.

CHAPTER 2:

OVERCOMING THE CULTURE OF HATE

Understanding What Drives Negativity and Jealousy in Others— and in Yourself

Okay, let's get into something real: negativity. We've all encountered it. Whether it's someone at work, a so-called "friend," or even random strangers online, there's always going to be someone who has something negative to say. And I know it's easy to point fingers and blame other people. But before we go down that road, let's pause for a second and ask ourselves: *Where does all of this negativity actually come from?*

I'll be the first to admit I've been on both sides of this. There was a time in my life when I felt like I had to put other people down to lift myself up. That might sound harsh, but it's true. I didn't realize it at the time, but negativity often stems from insecurities—either your own or someone else's. I remember when I was younger; there was this guy who always seemed to be one step ahead of me. He had the job I wanted, the car I dreamed of, the attention I thought I deserved. And instead of looking at that as inspiration, I felt a wave of jealousy that was hard to shake.

It wasn't that I didn't want to be happy for him, but I couldn't help but feel bitter because I wasn't where I thought I should be. It wasn't until later that I realized what I was really feeling wasn't hate—it was fear. I was afraid of being left behind, afraid that I wasn't enough, and that, somehow, I was falling short of the life I thought I should have.

The jealousy I felt wasn't about him at all—it was about me. It was a reflection of my own insecurities and unmet goals. So, if you've ever felt that way, trust me, you're not alone. The first step in overcoming jealousy is recognizing that those feelings usually have little to do with the other person and everything to do with how you're feeling about yourself.

Breaking Free from Toxic Cycles of Comparison and Criticism

Let's face it: comparing yourself to others is almost built into our DNA in this day and age. We're constantly surrounded by people's successes—on social media, at work, even in our personal lives. It's human nature to look at what others have and wonder, "Why don't I have that?" But here's the hard truth: comparison is one of the most toxic cycles you can get trapped in. It'll steal your peace, your joy, and your sense of self-worth if you let it.

I remember spending hours scrolling through social media, seeing people's vacation photos, their shiny new cars, their perfect families. At first, I'd smile and feel happy for them. But before I knew it, I'd start measuring my life against theirs. "Why aren't I doing that? Why can't I afford that? Why aren't my vacations that nice?" It was draining. I was so focused on other people's successes that I stopped appreciating my own progress.

The problem with comparison is that it's never an equal game. You're looking at someone's highlight reel, not their behind-the-scenes moments. You don't see the struggles, the sacrifices, or the challenges they're facing. They're probably looking at your life and thinking the same thing about you!

So, how do we break free from this cycle? It starts with shifting your mindset. Instead of focusing on other people's lives, start focusing on your own. I started making a conscious effort to celebrate my own victories, even the small ones, instead of obsessing over what others were doing. I started telling myself, "Your journey is yours alone, and there's no one else to compare it to." It was hard at first. I still struggled with feeling like I wasn't moving fast enough, but gradually, I began to feel more content with my own path.

A Real-Life Example: Getting Out of the Comparison Trap

Let me give you a personal example. A few years ago, I was working on a project that I knew could be a game-changer for my career. But instead of diving into the work, I spent hours on social media, comparing my progress to others. "Why hasn't anyone noticed me yet?" "How come so-and-so is getting more recognition?" All of these thoughts started to creep in, making me question whether I was even doing the right thing.

One night, I decided to get off social media and refocus. I took a deep breath and reminded myself: "This is *my* journey, not anyone else's." So, I refocused all of my energy on the project at hand. I stopped looking over my shoulder, stopped worrying about how other people were doing. And you know what happened? The project flourished. I got the recognition I deserved—not because I spent time comparing myself to others, but because I focused on my work and trusted that my efforts would pay off.

The truth is, the moment I let go of comparison, I was able to grow. I stopped competing with people who weren't even in the same race as me. And as a result, I started winning in my own way.

How to Stop Comparing Yourself to Others

✓ **Set personal goals, not comparative ones.** When you set goals, make sure they're aligned with *your* values and vision—not anyone else's. Forget about the next person's timeline. Focus on *your* next step. Ask yourself: "What do I want to achieve today, this week, this year?" Write it down, and make it your mission.

✓ **Stop scrolling.** Seriously. Social media is a highlight reel of everyone's best moments. It's not reality. So, if you find yourself feeling down after a scroll, it's time to step away. Give yourself permission to disconnect and focus on your own growth.

✓ *Celebrate your wins.* Start small. Did you finish that project you've been putting off? Celebrate it! Did you make progress toward a personal goal? Celebrate that, too. When you start recognizing and celebrating your wins, big or small, you'll start to notice that comparison doesn't have the same power over you.

✓ *Practice self-compassion.* We all have bad days. We all have moments when we feel like we're not enough. But don't beat yourself up for it. Instead, practice kindness toward yourself. Remind yourself that everyone has a unique journey, and you're doing the best you can with what you have.

Moving Forward: Letting Go of Jealousy and Embracing Your Own Path

Remember, jealousy is just a reflection of where you're feeling insecure. It's an opportunity to look inward and ask yourself: *What is it about this person's success that makes me feel threatened or less than?* The answer often lies in something you wish you had or something you want for yourself. So, instead of letting that jealousy fuel resentment, use it as fuel for your own growth. Let it remind you of what you want to achieve and use it as motivation to go after those dreams without looking at anyone else.

It's not easy. Trust me, I know. But once you learn to break free from the comparison trap, you'll find a feeling of peace and focus that's hard to describe. Instead of looking at others with envy, you'll look at them with gratitude for what they've taught you and with excitement for what you can achieve on your own terms.

Final Thoughts

The next time you feel that tug of jealousy, remember: it's not about them—it's about you. The journey to overcoming jealousy starts with understanding where it comes from and taking responsibility for your own growth. By focusing on your own path, celebrating your own progress, and learning to move past the distractions of comparison, you'll build a life that's rich with purpose and fulfillment.

Let's take back our peace, one step at a time. And remember—there's no need to compete with anyone but the person you were yesterday. Keep moving forward, and don't let anyone or anything hold you back.

CHAPTER 3:

BUILDING A HATER-FREE MINDSET

Practicing Gratitude and Positivity

Let's start with something simple but incredibly powerful: gratitude. It might sound a little cliché, but I'm telling you—it's one of the most effective tools I've used to build a hater-free mindset. Why? Because negativity thrives when we focus on what we don't have, what we've missed out on, or what someone else has that we feel we lack. But gratitude flips that script.

I'll be honest: there was a time when I struggled to focus on gratitude. I was constantly looking around at other people, thinking they had it better, thinking they were further along in their journey. It wasn't that I didn't appreciate the good things in my life—I just wasn't focused on them. My mind was more concerned with what I didn't have than what I did.

Then, one day, I realized nothing in my life was going to change until I started *actively* focusing on the positives, no matter how small they seemed. I didn't need a perfect life to be thankful for the moments that mattered. So, I started small—just three things a day. Maybe it was as simple as being grateful for a hot cup of coffee in the morning or for the support of a friend. I'd write them down. Over time, those small moments of gratitude built up into something much bigger.

I noticed that the more I practiced gratitude, the less I cared about the stuff I didn't have. My focus shifted to the good things in my life, and with that shift came a sense of peace. Gratitude is powerful because it keeps you in the present and helps you realize that, even when things don't look perfect, there's always something to be thankful for. When you focus on the positives, there's no space left for the bitterness or resentment that can come from jealousy or negativity.

Always Remember:

> *"Gratitude turns the noise down, so your soul can hear what's truly valuable." – Charles E Tyler*

Building a Positive Outlook

But gratitude isn't the only thing that helps you develop a hater-free mindset. You also need to intentionally cultivate positivity. This doesn't mean pretending everything is always great when it's not—it's about actively choosing how you want to respond to life's challenges. Life's going to throw curveballs at you. People are going to try to bring you down. But how you respond is everything.

I remember a time when I was facing a lot of criticism at work. Some of it was constructive, but a lot of it wasn't. It was hurtful, and, honestly, it made me question my abilities. But rather than letting it crush my spirit, I decided to approach it with a mindset shift. Instead of getting angry or defensive, I chose to look at it from a positive angle. "What can I learn from this?" I asked myself. "How can I grow from this experience?"

Changing my perspective didn't happen overnight, but over time, it became easier to find the silver lining in every situation. Whether it was feedback from a colleague or something I read online, I'd always try to see the opportunity for growth rather than focusing on the negativity. It wasn't about ignoring the bad—it was about finding the good, even in tough situations.

Now, when I face criticism or negativity, I don't internalize it. I acknowledge it, learn from it if there's something useful there, and move forward. Developing a positive mindset doesn't mean ignoring challenges—it means facing them head-on with the belief that you'll learn and grow from them.

Always Remember:

"The true power of positivity isn't pretending everything is perfect; it's believing you can handle anything with grace." – Charles E Tyler

Developing Resilience to Criticism and Hate

Here's something I've had to learn the hard way: *you can't control what people say about you.* You can't control how they see you. What you can control is how you respond. This is where resilience comes in. Resilience is the ability to take the hits, deal with the criticism, and keep moving forward without letting it break you down. It's something I had to develop over time, and I've found that resilience is the key to building a hater-free mindset.

Early in my career, I took every piece of criticism personally. If someone said something negative about me or my work, it felt like a direct attack on my worth. And I'll admit, it hurt. But over time, I learned that not all criticism is about *you*. It's about the other person's perspective, their expectations, or their own frustrations. Once I understood that, it became easier to brush off the negativity.

Resilience is all about keeping your emotional balance, no matter what's thrown your way. It's about *choosing* not to let the opinions of others define your worth. It's something I had to practice—every single day.

One of the ways I've built resilience is by reminding myself that not everyone's opinion matters. It's easier said than done, but the more I focused on my own growth, the less I cared about external judgment. I started to ask myself, "Is this criticism constructive? Is it helping me grow, or is it just noise?" If it wasn't constructive, I let it go. Simple as that.

Always Remember:

"Resilience isn't about avoiding the storm; it's about dancing in the rain and keeping your eyes on the horizon." – Charles E Tyler

Surrounding Yourself with Uplifting People

There's a saying I love: "You are the average of the five people you spend the most time with." This couldn't be more true when it comes to building a hater-free mindset. If you're constantly around people who complain, criticize, or bring negativity into your life, it's going to be hard to stay positive. But when you surround yourself with uplifting people—people who support you, encourage you, and want to see you succeed—it's easier to keep your focus on your goals and ignore the noise.

I remember one particular situation where I was struggling with negative energy from a certain group of people at work. They were always gossiping, always complaining, and it started to drain me. I realized I was letting their negativity affect my mood and my mindset. So, I made a conscious decision to distance myself. It wasn't easy, but once I surrounded myself with people who uplifted and encouraged me, everything changed. My mood lifted. My confidence grew. I realized that positive energy is contagious—and when you surround yourself with the right people, it's much easier to stay focused and motivated.

Take a look at the people in your life—your friends, family, colleagues. Are they the type of people who lift you up? Are they supporting your growth? If you find yourself surrounded by negativity, it might be time to reevaluate those relationships. You deserve to be around people who encourage your growth, celebrate your wins, and offer support when you need it. Let go of toxic relationships and make room for positive influences.

Always Remember:

> "Energy is contagious; surround yourself with those whose glow matches your own." – Charles E Tyler

How to Build Your Own Hater-Free Mindset

So now you've got the foundation. You understand the power of gratitude, positivity, resilience, and surrounding yourself with uplifting people. But how do you make these habits stick? Here's how I started and how you can too:

✓ **Start each day with gratitude:**
I begin every morning by thinking of three things I'm grateful for. Some days, it's big things—my family, my health, my work. Other days, it's as simple as a cup of coffee or a quiet moment to myself. This sets the tone for the rest of the day and helps me stay grounded.

✓ **Focus on the positive:**
When you're faced with a challenge or criticism, pause and ask yourself, "What can I learn from this?" Instead of getting defensive or upset, shift your perspective. See every challenge as an opportunity for growth.

✓ **Practice resilience:**
Don't let the negativity of others affect your sense of self-worth. Remind yourself that you control how you respond to criticism. Choose to focus on your goals and let everything else roll off your back.

✓ **Surround yourself with positive people:**
Take a look at your inner circle. Are these people lifting you up? Are they supporting your growth? If not, it's okay to distance yourself. Make room for people who inspire and motivate you.

✓ **Celebrate your wins, big and small:**
Whether it's finishing a project or just making it through the day with a positive attitude, take a moment to celebrate your progress. Gratitude and celebration keep the momentum going.

Final Thoughts: Building a Hater-Free Life

Building a hater-free mindset isn't about ignoring criticism or pretending everything is always perfect. It's about developing the resilience to face challenges head-on and understanding that not everyone's opinion about you matters. Not everyone is going to understand your path, and that's okay. As you embrace this mindset, you'll realize that the negativity or criticism from others doesn't have to hold weight in your life unless you give it that power.

Here's something I've learned on this journey: **living hater-free doesn't mean you won't ever face hate or criticism—it means you won't let it stop you**. The difference is in your response. A hater-free life is about protecting your peace, not allowing external forces to determine how you feel or how you move forward. It's a choice. It's the ability to rise above and keep going, regardless of the noise. It's about saying, "I hear you, but I'm focused on my path, and nothing is going to derail me from my goals."

When you start to live this way, you'll notice something incredible: people who were once quick to criticize, judge or hate start to lose their influence over you. They can no longer trigger your insecurities because you no longer seek their validation. The space they once occupied in your mind starts to shrink, and in its place, you make room for your own growth and happiness.

But this doesn't just happen overnight. It takes time, effort, and constant self-reminders that your worth isn't defined by other people's opinions. You have to commit to building your resilience, cultivating a positive mindset, and embracing the notion that you are worthy of success—just as you are. No approval needed. No external validation required.

Here's the real magic of a hater-free mindset: the more you practice protecting your peace, the more your confidence grows. The more you focus on your own journey and drown out the negativity, the more your goals come into focus. You start to live life on your terms, with clarity and intention. And as you keep doing this, you'll attract more of what you want—because the world naturally gravitates toward people who know their worth and stand strong in their truth.

When you let go of the need to compete with others or compare your journey to theirs, you free yourself to achieve greatness without the burden of unnecessary competition. You realize that success isn't about being better than someone else; it's about being the best version of yourself. And when you make peace with that, something amazing happens: you no longer need to fight for space in the world. Instead, you create your own space, and the world makes room for you.

In this process, you'll also find that the people who truly matter—the ones who lift you up, cheer for your success, and genuinely want to see you win—will begin to show up more in your life. These are the relationships worth investing in, the ones that will carry you forward, especially when times get tough.

It's not always easy, but it's worth it. And remember: you have the power to choose how you respond to hate, how you protect your peace, and how you build a life that reflects your true values. Stay centered, stay focused, and always keep moving forward.

A hater-free life is not a life without challenges. It's a life where you face those challenges with strength, grace, and the unwavering belief that nothing can stop you from reaching your potential. When you live a hater-free life, you're no longer letting the outside world dictate your happiness. Instead, you take control of your own narrative, your own happiness, and your own success.

CHAPTER 4:

THE POWER OF LOW-KEY: THRIVING IN SUBTLETY

Embracing Humility and Simplicity

In a world that loves to showcase success loudly and constantly, the real power often lies in embracing humility and simplicity. We're all familiar with the "loudest voice in the room" mentality, but I've learned that sometimes, the most impactful person is the one who doesn't need to shout to be heard.

I'll admit I've had my moments where I felt the pressure to show off what I was doing—whether it was my career, my personal achievements, or just the day-to-day wins that made me feel proud. But over time, I realized that living authentically, without seeking constant validation from others, was where I found my true sense of fulfillment. The quieter path isn't always the easiest, but it is by far the most rewarding.

A great way to think of this concept is through a word I've coined: **"subtle living."** It's about finding value in the quiet spaces and letting the small, meaningful moments count. Subtle living means acting with purpose but without needing to explain every step. It's the person who quietly works behind the scenes, knowing that true success doesn't need to be paraded around.

I think about this a lot when reflecting on my early career. I used to think that the more I said, the more people would notice my skills and contributions. But as time went on, I realized that the quieter I became about my own achievements, the more I attracted genuine recognition from people who respected the work I was doing—not the words I was saying. I embraced simplicity: less talk, more action. That's when I saw real growth in myself.

Living Authentically Without Seeking Constant Validation

We all crave validation—it's natural. We want to feel seen, appreciated, and understood. But when you constantly seek approval from others, you risk losing touch with your true self. I had to learn this lesson the hard way. For years, I sought validation through achievements, social media likes, or even through the approval of my colleagues and peers. It was exhausting. The more I sought others' approval, the less satisfied I became with myself.

The moment I shifted my focus inward was the moment everything changed. I realized I didn't need to prove anything to anyone. Instead, I started living for me—not for the praise, the likes, or the comments. When I started taking pride in my work *because I was proud of it*, not because I was looking for applause, things began to feel more genuine. I found peace in knowing that the work I was doing had value on its own.

Now, when I do something I'm proud of, I don't feel the need to share it with the world. I take a moment to acknowledge the accomplishment internally, and that feels *enough*. It's like a little self-award ceremony; no crowd needed. I call this approach **"internal glow."** It's the glow you feel when you know you're doing the right thing and living in alignment with your true self without needing anyone to notice or comment.

And trust me, when you stop seeking constant validation, something amazing happens: you free yourself from the exhaustion of always needing to be seen. You give yourself permission to just *be*, without the weight of the world's expectations on your shoulders.

How to Avoid Burnout by Staying Grounded

In this world that moves at a pace so fast it can feel like a constant race, staying grounded becomes not just important—it's essential. One of the biggest mistakes I've made in the past was pushing myself to the brink of burnout, trying to keep up with the pressure of being constantly on, constantly achieving, and constantly performing.

I thought that the key to success was always doing more, never resting, never pausing. I wanted to prove that I was capable of handling everything thrown my way. But what I learned the hard way was that constant action without balance leads to exhaustion. And the more I burned out, the less effective I became.

That's when I realized I needed to embrace a lifestyle of **"grounded-moving."** This new approach meant staying rooted in my core values, prioritizing my mental and physical health, and creating space for rest. Grounded-moving is about pushing forward with intention but knowing when to take a step back to recharge. It's about having the wisdom to know that working smarter, not harder, leads to longer-term success.

When I began to live this way, everything changed. I was more focused. I was more creative. I was more effective. But most importantly, I felt better. I wasn't constantly drained by the pressure to be busy. I understood that rest was part of the process, not a setback.

New Words to Live By

As we dive deeper into this lifestyle, here are a few new terms I want you to keep in mind as you walk this path of subtlety and authenticity:

✓ **Subtle living:** Finding value in the quiet spaces, focusing on doing the work without needing to announce it.

✓ **Internal glow:** The satisfaction you feel when you know you've done the work for yourself, not for the applause or external recognition.

✓ **Grounded-moving:** The act of making progress while staying deeply connected to your core values, understanding the importance of both action and rest.

✓ **Quiet-grind:** The power of staying focused and working consistently, even if others don't see the daily effort. It's the quiet dedication that leads to big results.

✓ **Stealth-mode success:** Achieving your goals without fanfare or noise. The kind of success that comes through hard work, resilience, and patience.

These terms are more than just new words; they represent a way of life—one where you thrive by embracing simplicity, staying authentic, and protecting your energy.

How to Start Living the Low-Key Lifestyle

It's time to put these concepts into action. Here's how you can start living the low-key lifestyle today:

✓ **Create quiet spaces:** Whether it's through journaling or meditating, make time for introspection. This will help you stay grounded and in touch with what truly matters to you.

✓ **Choose intentional goals:** Focus on what really aligns with your values. Don't get caught up in chasing trends or what others are doing. Set goals that bring you personal fulfillment, not just external success.

✓ **Give yourself permission to rest:** Burnout is real. Don't be afraid to take a step back when needed. Make rest part of your routine— don't see it as a luxury, but as a necessary component of your success.

✓ **Celebrate quietly:** Find joy in your victories without needing others to see them. Take pride in your achievements without announcing them to the world.

✓ **Focus on the long game:** Think beyond short-term recognition. Build your life and career for the long haul, knowing that true success takes time and patience.

In this chapter, we've explored how to thrive in subtlety—living authentically, embracing humility, and staying grounded without burning out. The power of low-key is in its quiet resilience. It's in knowing who you are, doing the work, and letting your results speak for themselves. Keep these principles in mind as you continue your journey, and trust that staying low-key will lead you to a life filled with purpose, peace, and success.

CHAPTER 5:

LIVING WITH INTENTIONALITY

Setting Meaningful Goals and Focusing on What Truly Matters

In a world that's constantly pulling us in different directions, it's easy to lose yourself in the chaos. These days, we're bombarded with expectations—everyone else's, society's, and even the ones we put on ourselves. We're told to be this, do that, achieve this, buy that. The pressure to keep up, fit in, and collect things just for the status can get overwhelmingly fast.

But here's the truth. If you're not living intentionally, you'll end up drifting, chasing things that look good on the outside but don't bring real fulfillment.

I've been there. There were times I felt like I was working hard but going nowhere, spinning my wheels while life passed by. And honestly? Sometimes, I still feel like I'm not entirely living the life I imagine for myself. But I'm also deeply thankful for how far I've come. The shift didn't happen overnight. It began when I became honest with myself and started setting goals that truly aligned with who I am and what I value.

Living intentionally means choosing how you spend your time, energy, and focus. It's about figuring out what really matters to you and letting go of everything that doesn't serve your peace or your purpose. Once you start moving from that place, the noise quiets down. The pressure eases up. You stop chasing everyone else's version of success and start defining it for yourself.

The Importance of Self-Reflection

One of the most powerful practices I've adopted in my life is self-reflection. Without taking the time to reflect on where I am, where I've been, and where I want to go, I found it hard to make the right decisions. Self-reflection helps you gain clarity about your goals and values, making it easier to live intentionally.

You don't need to wait for the new year to start reflecting. Reflection can be done anytime. I set aside time each week to ask myself simple, but important, questions like:

What did I accomplish this week that aligns with my goals?

What areas of my life need more attention or improvement?

What is draining my energy, and how can I set boundaries to protect myself?

These questions help me stay on track and ensure that I'm moving forward with purpose. Reflection isn't about beating yourself up; it's about checking in with yourself and ensuring that your actions align with your values and long-term vision.

Creating a Vision for Your Life

When was the last time you really thought about the bigger picture of your life? Too often, we get caught up in the daily grind and forget to pause and ask ourselves, *What do I want my life to look like in five, ten, or twenty years?* Creating a vision for your life is one of the most powerful things you can do. It gives you a sense of purpose and direction and helps you focus on what really matters.

I spent years trying to live up to other people's expectations of success. I thought success was about having a title, a certain amount of money, or a fancy car. But over time, I realized that success, for me, isn't about what others think. It's about feeling fulfilled in the life I'm creating. That's why creating a personal vision was so important. Once I defined my vision, I knew exactly what to focus on, and it made all of my decisions easier.

A vision doesn't have to be a grand, unattainable dream. It can be as simple as "I want to live a balanced life where I prioritize my health, my family, and my personal growth" or "I want to build a career that allows me to make a positive impact." Whatever your vision is, make sure it's something that feels authentic to you.

How to Set Meaningful Goals

Once you have a clear vision, it's time to turn that vision into actionable goals. But not just any goals—meaningful goals that align with your values and aspirations.

I used to set goals based on what I thought I should do or what others were doing. These goals were often based on external measures of success, like "get promoted" or "buy a bigger house." But, after realizing that these goals weren't fulfilling for me, I shifted to setting goals that were truly meaningful and aligned with my own vision.

Here's how to set meaningful goals:

✓ **Be specific**
Vague goals like "get healthier" or "make more money" don't give you a clear direction. Instead, make your goals specific. For example, "Lose 10 pounds in 6 months by exercising three times a week and eating healthier." This gives you a clear path to follow.

✓ **Break down big goals into smaller steps**
Large goals can feel overwhelming. Break them down into smaller, manageable steps. If your goal is to write a book, start by setting smaller goals like "write 500 words a day" or "complete one chapter per month."

✓ **Set a timeline**
Without a timeline, goals can get pushed aside. Set realistic deadlines for each goal, but make sure they're flexible enough to accommodate life's inevitable setbacks.

✓ **Make them measurable**
It's essential to track your progress. For example, if your goal is to save money, track how much you're saving each month and adjust your budget accordingly. This helps you stay motivated and see your progress.

✓ **Align them with your values**
Your goals should align with what truly matters to you. Ask yourself: *Does this goal bring me closer to the life I want to create?* If not, it's time to reassess.

The Power of Saying No: Making Peace with Prioritizing Yourself

Living intentionally also means learning how to say no. Saying no is one of the most powerful ways to protect your time, energy, and peace. We're all guilty of saying yes to things we don't really want to do— whether it's social obligations, extra work, or activities that drain us.

I used to say yes to everything, trying to please everyone. But what I realized is that by saying yes to things that didn't serve me, I was saying no to the things that truly mattered. Saying no doesn't make you selfish—it makes you intentional. It allows you to prioritize your goals, your health, and your well-being.

Here's how you can start saying no:

✓ **Know your priorities**
Understand what's most important to you. When you have a clear vision and set goals, it becomes easier to say no to things that don't align with your values.

✓ **Practice saying no politely**
Saying no doesn't have to be rude. You can simply say, "Thank you for the invitation, but I have other commitments that I need to focus on." It's about protecting your time without feeling guilty.

✓ **Recognize your limits**
You don't have to do everything. Recognize when you're stretching yourself too thin and make a conscious choice to step back. It's okay to take a break or pass on something that doesn't serve you.

✓ **Give yourself permission**
Understand that it's okay to say no. You don't have to explain yourself or feel bad for taking care of your needs. When you prioritize yourself, you're in a better position to help others.

The Importance of Setting Boundaries

Boundaries are crucial when it comes to living with intention. Without them, it's easy to get pulled in too many directions. Boundaries help you protect your time, energy, and emotional well-being so you can focus on what truly matters.

In my life, setting boundaries has been key to maintaining my peace. Whether it's with family, friends, or colleagues, I've learned that it's okay to set limits. I set boundaries around my work hours, my personal time, and even my emotional energy. Boundaries are about saying, "This is where I draw the line," and respecting your own needs.

Setting boundaries is an act of self-care. It helps you stay aligned with your goals and avoid burnout. It's about creating space for the things that matter most and letting go of things that drain you.

Final Thoughts: Living with Intentionality Every Day

Living with intentionality isn't just about setting goals—it's about making every decision with purpose. It's about aligning your actions with your values and ensuring that the path you're walking leads you toward a life that's fulfilling and meaningful.

The key to living intentionally is self-awareness. It's knowing what truly matters to you and being willing to say no to things that don't align with your vision. It's about being mindful of where you invest your time and energy and choosing to focus on what will bring you the most joy and fulfillment.

When you live intentionally, you don't waste time chasing after things that don't serve you. You stop living for the approval of others and start living for yourself. You make decisions that bring you closer to your dreams and help you build a life that reflects your true values. This is how you build a life of meaning and purpose—by living with intention every single day.

"Intentional living is the art of aligning your actions with your values, creating a life that is uniquely yours and free from the noise of external expectations." – Charles E Tyler

CHAPTER 6:

SOCIAL MEDIA: NAVIGATING THE NOISE

Staying Low-Key and Hater-Free in a World Obsessed with Likes, Shares, and Viral Moments

Let's be real for a second: we live in a world obsessed with social media. Whether it's Instagram, Facebook, TikTok, Twitter, or whatever new platform is trending, it's easy to get caught up in the endless cycle of likes, shares, and viral moments. It can feel like there's an unspoken pressure to constantly post, update your status, or share your every move with the world. And if you're not sharing every part of your life, are you even really *living*?

I know I've felt that pressure before. There was a time when I used social media almost like a badge of honor. I was constantly checking for likes, making sure I was in the loop with trending topics, and trying to keep up with what everyone else was doing. It was exhausting. And, to be honest, it was distracting me from the things that really mattered.

Social media has a way of making us feel like we have to *show up* in a certain way. Like our lives need to be curated for an audience, as though the only way to feel validated is to have others approve of what we post. But here's the thing: the moment we start living for social media's approval, we lose sight of our true selves. I realized I needed to pull back from the constant noise and refocus on what truly mattered to me—my goals, my values, and my peace.

It wasn't easy. The temptation to scroll endlessly was always there. But slowly, I began to distance myself from the need for validation from others. I stopped checking my phone every five minutes, I stopped comparing my posts to others', and, most importantly, I started sharing less. I focused on being present rather than constantly trying to prove I was having a perfect life. And let me tell you—letting go of the social media "performance" was one of the most freeing decisions I ever made.

"In a world that thrives on the loudest voice, choose the quiet power of presence over the noise of validation." – Charles E Tyler

Creating Healthy Boundaries with Technology

One of the most crucial steps I took in reclaiming my peace was setting clear boundaries with technology, especially social media. Social media is a tool, but it can easily become a source of anxiety if we're not mindful of how we use it. For years, I was hooked. My phone was my constant companion, and I'd check it as soon as I woke up and right before bed. Social media was in my hands, in my mind, and on my schedule. But over time, I realized how much it was draining me.

The moment I started setting boundaries, things changed. I decided to turn off notifications for apps like Instagram and Facebook. I also set specific times during the day to check my messages and posts, and I made it a habit to keep my phone out of reach when I was spending time with loved ones. I also decided to stay off social media for at least an hour after I woke up, giving myself time to focus on my day without the external distractions of other people's lives. These small changes made a big difference in how I felt about myself and how I approached the day ahead.

The key to managing social media is learning that *you are in control*. It's easy to get sucked into the constant flow of information, but when you take a step back and set healthy boundaries, you regain control over your own time and mental space. Technology is a tool, but you are the one who decides how and when to use it.

You don't have to be on every platform or constantly check your notifications. You don't owe anyone an update on your life. Social media doesn't define you, and it doesn't have to consume your thoughts. By setting boundaries, you allow yourself the freedom to live your life without the weight of comparison, distraction, or pressure.

"Technology is a tool, not a tether. Don't let it define your worth or your reality." – Charles E Tyler

Why It's Okay to Share Less

Now, let's talk about something that might feel counterintuitive: *It's okay to share less.* We're in a culture that celebrates oversharing—telling the world everything you're doing, eating, thinking. But I've learned that sharing less doesn't make you less connected. In fact, it often creates deeper connections because you're focusing on what really matters, not the constant need for validation.

I've had to remind myself that social media is just a snapshot of a much larger picture. It's not real life. It's curated. It's filtered. And often, it's a distorted reflection of what someone wants the world to see. When I realized that, I began to feel less pressure to post and share everything I was doing. I didn't need to tell the world about every little accomplishment or update. Instead, I began sharing things that truly mattered to me and those closest to me. And when I did share, it was from a place of authenticity, not to keep up with some arbitrary standard.

By sharing less, I was able to focus more on the real, meaningful connections in my life. I didn't need to constantly prove myself to an online audience. I could just be. And that's one of the most powerful shifts you can make in today's social media-driven world—knowing that your worth isn't tied to your digital footprint.

"True connection doesn't come from the number of likes you get, but from the depth of the relationships you build offline."
Charles E Tyler

How to Navigate Social Media and Stay Low-Key

So, how do we stay low-key and hater-free while navigating the noise of social media? It's all about *intentionality* and *balance*. Here's how I've learned to manage the digital world without losing my peace:

✓ **Limit your screen time**
Set boundaries around how much time you spend on social media. Use your phone's built-in features to track screen time or set daily limits for apps. By doing this, you can protect your mental space from unnecessary distractions.

✓ **Unfollow what doesn't serve you**
Be intentional about who and what you follow. If someone's posts leave you feeling jealous, anxious, or less-than, it's okay to unfollow them. Protect your energy and only engage with content that inspires, uplifts, or educates you.

✓ **Avoid scrolling first thing in the morning**
This was a big one for me. Instead of grabbing my phone as soon as I wake up, I decided to spend the first hour of my day without the distraction of social media. This time is now dedicated to focusing on myself—whether it's reading, journaling, or simply enjoying a peaceful breakfast.

✓ **Practice mindful posting**
When you do share something, make sure it's for the right reasons. Ask yourself: "Am I sharing this to inspire or connect, or am I just seeking validation?" Sharing with purpose and authenticity brings more satisfaction than posting just for the sake of it.

✓ **Engage thoughtfully**
Social media is a tool for connection, but it's easy to fall into the trap of superficial engagement. Instead of mindlessly scrolling or liking everything that comes your way, take the time to engage thoughtfully with posts that matter to you. Leave meaningful

comments, share advice, or simply show support in a way that adds value to someone else's experience.

Final Thoughts: The Power of Navigating the Noise

Social media is undeniably one of the most powerful tools of our time. It has the ability to connect us, inspire us, and even change lives for the better. However, as we all know, it can also lead us down a path of comparison, anxiety, and even despair if we're not careful. We see people posting their best moments, their highlights, and their successes, and it's easy to fall into the trap of thinking we're not enough. The truth is, social media can sometimes create a distorted reality that we unknowingly measure ourselves against.

I'm sure you've heard stories or even personally witnessed how social media can contribute to mental health struggles. The constant pressure to present a "perfect" life, the relentless comparison to others, and the obsession with likes, follows, and approval can all pile up. I've seen people hit rock bottom after years of struggling with the toxic side of social media. From people getting trapped in the cycle of unrealistic beauty standards to feeling inadequate because their accomplishments don't seem to measure up to those of their peers — it's clear that the impact of social media is no small matter.

But here's the thing: **social media is not inherently bad.** It's a tool. And just like any tool, it can be used in ways that either harm us or help us, depending on how we approach it. The challenge is learning to navigate it with mindfulness and intention. It's about understanding that social media, like any other tool, should be used in a way that enhances our lives, not diminishes them. We have to be careful, cognizant, and intentional with how we engage with the digital world.

Think about it. Social media can be a powerful platform for spreading positivity, raising awareness, building communities, and sharing knowledge. It can connect people from across the world, give a voice to the voiceless, and inspire others to take action. There are countless examples of individuals and organizations using social media for social good—whether it's raising funds for a cause, supporting mental health awareness, or providing educational content that helps people learn and grow.

Yet, while there are many great things social media can do, we also need to protect our peace. We need to find balance. It's easy to get caught up in the whirlwind of likes, comments, and followers, but that doesn't define your worth. You are so much more than your online persona. Your life, your accomplishments, and your happiness don't have to be validated by how many people engage with your posts. The true value of your life is not measured by social media metrics but by the real, meaningful moments you create offline—the relationships you nurture, the work you do, and the impact you have in the lives of those around you.

I've had my own battles with social media. There were times when I let it distract me from what really mattered, when I let other people's highlights make me question my own path. But over time, I learned to use social media intentionally. I started curating my feeds to inspire me, to educate me, and to connect me with people who shared my values. I made a conscious decision to follow accounts that uplifted me, that contributed to my growth, and that supported my well-being. It wasn't easy to break away from the comparison game, but as I did, I found more clarity in my own life.

Here's where we need to be mindful: **social media can either contribute to our mental well-being or be a source of stress—it's up to us how we use it.** This doesn't mean we have to completely disconnect or avoid it. But it does mean we need to set boundaries. We need to decide what we want to see, what we want to engage with, and how we want to spend our time online. Make sure that your online world reflects the life you want to live—one that's positive, empowering, and focused on your personal growth.

Social media can be a tool for connection, but it can also be a tool for disconnection if we're not careful. The more we focus on the highlights of others, the further we get from our own authentic experiences. So, take a moment and reflect on what your social media usage is contributing to your life. Is it fueling your growth, or is it draining you? Is it bringing you closer to the people and values you care about, or is it pulling you into comparison and negativity?

Here's the challenge I want to leave you with: **Use social media as a tool for the greater good, for your own well-being, and for connecting with others in meaningful ways.** Share what uplifts you, celebrate the small wins, and connect with people who inspire you to be the best version of yourself. Be intentional. Don't live for the likes. Live for the real moments, the real connections, and the real growth you experience every day.

And most importantly, **remember that social media is just one part of the picture—it's not the whole picture.** True happiness, fulfillment, and success come from living authentically, from nurturing your relationships offline, and from creating a life that feels aligned with your values and dreams. Let's not get lost in the noise of comparison. Instead, let's use social media as a tool to amplify what truly matters and to connect with people who elevate us.

"Social media should never be a reflection of your worth; let it be a mirror of your intention." – Charles E Tyler

CHAPTER 7:

CREATING A LOW-KEY, HATER-FREE COMMUNITY

In today's world, it's easy to get caught up in negativity, competition, and the pressures of comparison. Social media, in particular, often exacerbates this by providing a constant stream of "highlight reels" from people's lives—vacations, promotions, relationships, and achievements. These snippets can make us feel as though everyone around us is living a life we should aspire to. We find ourselves comparing our behind-the-scenes to their public moments, which often leads to feelings of inadequacy, envy, and discontent. But true success is not found in tearing others down—it's found in lifting one another up.

Creating a low-key, hater-free community is about more than just avoiding drama; it's about actively cultivating a space where positivity, respect, and personal growth are the driving forces. In a world that thrives on the sensational, we have the power to build communities that celebrate the simple, authentic, and unpretentious. These communities aren't focused on the latest trends or the next big thing, but instead on supporting each other through real, meaningful connections. Here, success is not measured by external validation or fleeting achievements but by the depth of our relationships and the strength of our collective spirit.

This mindset requires us to shift our focus away from external competition and comparison. Rather than viewing others' success as something to envy or even diminish, we start to see it as a reflection of what's possible for all of us. Success in this kind of community is not a zero-sum game. When one person succeeds, we all succeed. We realize that helping someone else succeed doesn't take away from our own journey—in fact, it often propels us forward. When we lift up others, we create a ripple effect that helps us all grow.

Building a low-key, hater-free community is also about showing up for each other in real, tangible ways. It's about being there when things get tough, as much as when things are going well. True support isn't just about applauding someone's success; it's about being there during their struggles. It's offering a listening ear, a helping hand, or just showing up when no one else does. These acts of kindness and empathy are what bind communities together. They create trust, and trust is the foundation upon which great relationships are built. Without trust, communities fall apart, but when it's cultivated, it becomes the bedrock of everything else.

In a world that often pushes us toward competition and comparison, genuine relationships help us return to what truly matters— connection, empathy, and shared purpose. These relationships are what give us the strength to keep going when we feel discouraged. They provide the kind of emotional safety and stability that allow us to pursue our dreams without fear of failure or ridicule. In a low-key, hater-free community, people encourage one another, not tear each other down. And while personal achievements are celebrated, the focus remains on the collective success of the community as a whole.

Inspiring Others to Embrace Positivity and Mindfulness

Positivity and mindfulness aren't just buzzwords—they're powerful tools that can completely transform the way we live and interact with others. When you choose positivity, you're not ignoring the hard parts of life; you're choosing to focus on the solutions and lessons rather than the problems. This mindset doesn't just help you cope with challenges, but it also spreads to the people around you.

When you begin to lead with positivity, you create an atmosphere that encourages others to do the same. A person who radiates positivity naturally attracts those who are looking for encouragement, inspiration, and a sense of peace. Your behavior becomes an invitation for others to embrace their own growth and potential. When we surround ourselves with individuals who focus on solutions rather than dwelling on difficulties, it creates an environment of growth and opportunity.

Positivity also begins with mindfulness. Being mindful means being present in the moment, understanding your thoughts and emotions, and choosing your responses consciously. This practice can be life-changing when it comes to building stronger communities because it encourages better communication and deeper empathy. Instead of reacting impulsively or harshly, mindfulness teaches you to pause, reflect, and choose your actions wisely.

How You Can Inspire Positivity:

✓ **Lead by Example:** People are influenced by actions more than words. When you show up with a positive attitude, it sets the tone for others to follow. A smile, a word of encouragement, or even a kind gesture can make a world of difference.

✓ **Focus on Gratitude:** Practice gratitude daily, and share it with others. Whether it's in a group chat or face-to-face, expressing what you're thankful for can shift the group's mindset toward the positive. This helps to reframe challenges as opportunities rather than setbacks.

✓ **Be a Problem Solver, Not a Complainer:** It's easy to complain about what's wrong, but true leaders focus on how things can improve. When someone shares a problem, offer solutions or at least a plan to work together to figure it out. This mindset helps everyone in the community stay solution-oriented.

✓ **Encourage Growth in Others:** Instead of getting jealous or threatened by another person's success, celebrate it. Lift others up and encourage them to continue growing. When people feel supported in their journeys, they are more likely to reciprocate that support.

✓ By making positivity and mindfulness a core part of your interactions, you encourage a ripple effect that can change the dynamic of an entire community. People will feel empowered, respected, and inspired to do their best, not out of competition, but out of mutual respect and shared growth.

Building Stronger, More Genuine Relationships

The foundation of any successful community is the strength of its relationships. Relationships are the glue that holds people together through thick and thin. They are the bridges that connect us when we feel isolated and the pillars of support when we face difficulties. It's important to understand that genuine, strong relationships don't just happen by chance—they require intentional effort, trust, and nurturing. Too often, we get caught up in the notion that more connections are better. We focus on the number of friends, followers, or acquaintances we have rather than the depth of those relationships. It's tempting to collect people in our lives as if they were trophies or statistics, measuring our worth by how many people we know. But quantity doesn't guarantee quality. The real value of relationships comes from the connection we build with others, not from the sheer number of people we interact with.

True success in community-building isn't about having a large circle; it's about having a few key people in your corner who genuinely care about you and want to see you succeed. These are the people who will stand by you through the highs and lows, who offer guidance when needed and provide encouragement without hesitation. A smaller circle of trusted, supportive individuals can offer much more in terms of personal growth and emotional security than a large group of superficial relationships.

To build a low-key, hater-free community, you need to start with relationships that are rooted in trust, mutual respect, and an authentic desire to support each other. A community based on these values allows people to thrive, as it cultivates an environment where people feel safe enough to be vulnerable and to grow without fear of judgment. Strong relationships are not transactional—they're not about what you can take from someone, but rather about what you can offer and how you can help each other. It's about being there for people, not only when they're at their best, but also when they are at their lowest. When a community is built on this kind of support, it becomes a force that can overcome anything.

In a world that often pushes us toward competition and comparison, genuine relationships help us return to what truly matters—connection, empathy, and shared purpose. These relationships are what give us the strength to keep going when we feel discouraged. They provide the kind of emotional safety and stability that allow us to pursue our dreams without fear of failure or ridicule. In a low-key, hater-free community, people encourage one another, not tear each other down. And while personal achievements are celebrated, the focus remains on the collective success of the community as a whole.

The Crab in the Barrel Mentality

In many communities, there's a subtle but powerful force that hinders progress and stifles growth: the "crab in the barrel" mentality. This is when individuals or groups, rather than lifting each other up, pull one another down in an effort to keep everyone at the same level. Picture this: a barrel filled with crabs. Each time one attempts to climb out and escape, the others grab hold and drag it back down. This mentality is not only toxic, but it also prevents growth, advancement, and success. It's the fear of someone else's success that holds people back, even if that success has nothing to do with their own journey.

The "crab in the barrel" mentality thrives on jealousy, insecurity, and competition. Instead of working together to build something greater, there's an unspoken fear that helping someone else will somehow diminish your own value. When you start focusing on your own personal growth and encouraging others to do the same, you break free from this destructive cycle.

How to Break the Cycle:

✓ **Embrace the Growth of Others:** Realize that someone else's success doesn't take anything away from you. Celebrate the wins of others as if they were your own, because in doing so, you foster a spirit of support and camaraderie.

✓ **Cultivate a Positive Mindset:** Don't let envy or jealousy dictate your actions. Instead of competing with others, focus on improving yourself. Personal growth is the most fulfilling kind of progress, and when you focus on yourself, you naturally inspire others to do the same.

✓ **Collaborate, Don't Compete:** Look for opportunities to work together, not against each other. Collaboration is one of the most powerful ways to multiply success. When you combine your talents with others, you can achieve so much more than you ever could on your own.

Being Pretentious Isn't Good Either

While it's important to avoid the crab-in-the-barrel mentality, there's another pitfall that some fall into: trying to keep up with the Joneses. In today's world, with social media constantly showing curated highlights of others' lives, it's easy to get caught up in the pressure to appear successful, stylish, or wealthy. But living a life focused on keeping up appearances, or being pretentious, can be incredibly harmful—not only to your mental well-being but also to your financial stability.

Trying to outdo others with material possessions or extravagant lifestyles doesn't lead to true happiness or fulfillment. It can often push you into unnecessary debt and stress. In the pursuit of a status you don't need, you might end up compromising your financial health, your values, and your peace of mind. Keeping up with the Joneses can seem attractive on the surface, but it's built on the belief that worth is measured by what we have, rather than who we are.

The reality is that this kind of mentality doesn't contribute to building a low-key, hater-free community. It breeds insecurity, competition, and jealousy, as people try to keep up with others' expectations instead of focusing on their own goals. When you focus on living authentically and prioritizing what truly matters, you create an environment where people can thrive at their own pace without the pressure to perform for others.

How to Avoid the Pitfalls of Pretentiousness:

✓ **Live Within Your Means:** Avoid the temptation to overspend to impress others. Financial health comes from living within your means, making conscious decisions about where you invest your money, and focusing on experiences and personal growth rather than material possessions.

✓ **Prioritize Personal Growth:** True success isn't about what you have; it's about who you are becoming. Invest in yourself—your skills, your knowledge, your emotional well-being—rather than spending to appear successful.

✓ **Embrace Authenticity:** Instead of trying to keep up with others, embrace your own journey and successes. Be proud of your personal accomplishments, even if they look different from what others are doing. Authenticity leads to true confidence.

Building Together for Mutual Growth

When we step away from the crab-in-the-barrel mentality and begin working together, we open up the opportunity for mutual growth. Success isn't a zero-sum game—it's something that can benefit everyone involved. In a world that often pits us against each other, it's easy to forget that collaboration is far more powerful than competition. Think of success as a shared goal, where everyone contributes and everyone benefits. When we bring our resources, talents, and knowledge together, we can build something far more powerful than what we could ever create individually.

The power of a united community isn't just in the big moments—it's in the collective effort. Everyone's contribution matters, and by working together, we amplify each other's strengths. Success becomes a shared journey, not a race to the top. By pooling our skills and resources, we multiply our efforts and maximize the potential for success, not just for ourselves, but for everyone involved.

Final Thoughts: The Power of Unity Over Jealousy

In the end, a low-key, hater-free community is one that understands the value of working together. It's not just about avoiding drama or toxicity—it's about a fundamental shift in how we perceive success and collaboration. When we stop viewing life as a race, and instead embrace the idea that success is not a solitary pursuit, we begin to see the true power of community. Unity isn't about creating a competition to see who's "better"; it's about recognizing that each individual's growth contributes to the strength of the whole. A community that thrives on unity and support is a place where everyone feels empowered to succeed, not in isolation, but together.

Unity requires us to recognize the collective strength we have when we support one another. It's easy to fall into the trap of comparison, especially in a world so hyper-connected by social media, but when we embrace unity, we free ourselves from the pressures of competition and jealousy. Success isn't a finite resource—it's a mindset. There's no shortage of it. In fact, the more we lift one another up, the more success is multiplied. We find strength not just in our own achievements, but in seeing others win. This mindset shift creates a space where we are genuinely happy for each other's victories because we understand that someone else's success doesn't take anything away from ours. Instead, it expands the idea that success is something that can benefit everyone involved.

When we celebrate each other's wins, we take part in something bigger than ourselves. We're no longer just a collection of individuals trying to outdo one another, but a collective force, supporting and encouraging one another to be the best versions of ourselves. That's the beauty of a low-key, hater-free community. It's a space where people can thrive not by stepping on others, but by creating an environment where everyone has the resources, encouragement, and belief in themselves to succeed.

In such a community, every person's growth becomes an opportunity for the entire group to evolve. We understand that growth is contagious. One person's success can inspire and motivate others to push through their own challenges. That's the ripple effect of unity: it starts with one person's courage to rise, and it spreads, affecting everyone around them. When we collaborate, we don't just help one person at a time—we lift the entire community.

This community mindset doesn't just benefit the individuals involved—it benefits society as a whole. When we make the conscious choice to prioritize collaboration over competition, we begin to shift the culture. Instead of tearing each other down, we create a culture that celebrates the diversity of talents, skills, and experiences that each person brings to the table. We recognize that our individual strengths combine to form something far greater than what we could achieve alone. The support we offer one another creates a foundation for a stronger, more resilient community. And as we build that foundation, we create a model for others to follow.

By coming together, we not only build stronger communities, but we also contribute to a more positive, supportive world. We send a message that collaboration is more powerful than rivalry, and that mutual success is something to be celebrated, not feared. As we encourage one another to reach for new heights, we pave the way for future generations to do the same. This is how we shift the focus from a world of division to one where everyone has the opportunity to thrive, regardless of their background, resources, or circumstances.

When we take the time to foster an environment of trust, respect, and collaboration, we begin to see the profound impact it has, not just within our communities, but in the world beyond. A low-key, hater-free community doesn't just provide opportunities for individuals to succeed—it creates a ripple of change that can influence larger systems, reshape industries, and lead to societal transformation. We create a world where success is not an isolated event, but a collective experience that fosters innovation, connection, and progress.

By putting unity over jealousy, we do more than just build a supportive community—we build a foundation for long-term growth, empowerment, and sustainability. The more we work together, the stronger we become. Success is no longer measured by how far we can climb individually, but by how many people we can help rise with us. This is the essence of a low-key, hater-free community—a community that thrives, grows, and succeeds together, creating lasting change and leaving a positive mark on the world.

> *"Unity is the most powerful force in any community. When we embrace it, success becomes limitless, and the impact we have together will change the world, one step at a time."*
> *Charles E Tyler*

CHAPTER 8:

CONCLUSION: MASTERING THE ART OF LIVING UNBOTHERED

As we reach the final chapter of this journey together, I want you to pause and reflect on everything we've discussed. Living a low-key, hater-free life isn't just a goal—it's an art. It's a way of living that requires intentional effort, self-awareness, and a deep commitment to cultivating positivity and growth within yourself and your community. The principles we've covered in these pages are designed not only to help you create a life free of negativity, but to guide you toward a mindset that fosters unity, support, and success for all.

The foundation of living unbothered starts with your own inner peace. Too often, we let the noise of the world, the opinions of others, and the pressure of comparison dictate how we feel about ourselves. But when you embrace the art of living unbothered, you reclaim your power. You stop allowing the external world to shape your worth. Instead, you define your own success, grounded in your values, your purpose, and your community.

Living unbothered isn't about being indifferent to the world around you; it's about choosing how you engage with it. It's about having the emotional resilience to rise above drama, criticism, and negativity. It's about knowing when to step back, when to let go, and when to stay focused on what truly matters. It's the ability to rise above the small stuff and make space for the big things: personal growth, meaningful relationships, and a life filled with purpose.

A key aspect of mastering this art is learning to filter out the noise. There will always be distractions—people, opinions, and external pressures that seek to pull you off course. But when you build a solid foundation of self-worth and a low-key, hater-free community, you begin to develop the strength to block out that noise. You become less affected by what others say or think and more focused on your own journey and the positive impact you can make.

The power of this mindset is immeasurable. Imagine a world where everyone embraced the art of living unbothered. A world where people focused on their own growth, supported one another, and celebrated each other's successes without jealousy or competition. It would be a world of collaboration, support, and shared success—a world where everyone can thrive, without the weight of comparison or negativity.

Living with Purpose and Intentionality

As we've discussed in previous chapters, intentionality is key to this lifestyle. Living with purpose isn't about setting a million goals or trying to keep up with the Joneses—it's about aligning your actions with your values. It's about knowing where you're going and making every decision with intention, rather than being swept away by external forces. When you live intentionally, you invest your time, energy, and focus into what truly matters, and you stop wasting time on things that don't align with your mission.

This sense of purpose fuels your growth. It gives you direction and clarity, so that when challenges arise, you can approach them with confidence and resilience. When you know who you are and where you're headed, distractions and negativity become less impactful. You don't have to engage in every drama or chase every opportunity—only the ones that truly serve your vision and goals.

One of the most powerful aspects of living with intention is the freedom it provides. When you stop living for the approval of others and start living for yourself, you free yourself from the chains of comparison, jealousy, and insecurity. You can walk through life knowing that you're doing what feels right for you, not what others think is right for you. This autonomy is liberating, and it's what makes the art of living unbothered so powerful.

Mastering Your Emotional Landscape

The key to living unbothered also lies in mastering your emotional landscape. This means developing emotional intelligence—the ability to recognize, understand, and manage your emotions, as well as those of others. Emotional intelligence allows you to navigate life's ups and downs with grace, responding to challenges with calm and clarity rather than reacting impulsively or letting external factors dictate your mood.

When you master your emotions, you become less reactive and more proactive. You stop letting negativity and drama pull you into unhealthy patterns of thought and behavior. Instead, you learn to create space between stimulus and response, giving yourself time to choose how you want to react. This emotional mastery empowers you to stay grounded, even in the face of adversity.

Living unbothered doesn't mean suppressing your emotions or pretending everything is okay when it's not—it's about acknowledging your feelings without letting them control you. It's about recognizing when something or someone is trying to trigger you, and choosing to rise above it. When you develop this emotional awareness, you create an inner peace that is unshakable, no matter what's going on around you.

Creating a Community of Like-Minded People

Another cornerstone of living unbothered is the community you surround yourself with. As we've explored, a low-key, hater-free community is one that fosters support, collaboration, and shared growth. But to create this kind of environment, you must first become intentional about the people you invite into your life.

A community of like-minded people will elevate your mindset, support your goals, and help you stay on track when things get tough. These people are the ones who believe in your vision and encourage your success without trying to compete or bring you down. They celebrate your wins and are there for you when you face setbacks. A community like this is the foundation of your ability to thrive and live unbothered.

Surround yourself with individuals who inspire you, challenge you, and support you. These people won't try to diminish your success—they'll help amplify it. When you find and build this kind of community, you begin to see the profound impact it has on your own life and well-being. It's a powerful reminder that success is not a solo journey but something that we achieve together.

The Ripple Effect of Living Unbothered

Finally, living unbothered has a ripple effect. When you embrace this mindset, you not only change your own life, but you influence those around you. People notice your calm, your focus, and your positivity, and they're drawn to it. You become a model of resilience and grace, showing others that it's possible to thrive without drama, competition, or jealousy.

This ripple effect extends beyond your immediate community. It affects your work, your relationships, and your broader social circles. When you live unbothered, you set a new standard for how people should treat one another. You create a space where people can express themselves authentically, celebrate each other's successes, and support each other's growth. The world needs more of this—more unity, more collaboration, and more people who are committed to living with purpose and authenticity.

Final Quote:

"Living low-key and hater-free is the art of choosing peace over chaos, unity over division, and growth over comparison. It's not just about being undisturbed; it's about creating a world where everyone has the space to thrive." – Charles E Tyler

CHAPTER 9:
LOW KEY & HATER-FREE
THE BIBLICAL BLUEPRINT

S ometimes, I sit back and think, "Maybe this is just saying that sounds good because it rhymes, has a vibe, *and is just something to share amongst friends from time to time."*

However, the truth is that God has been moving in this way, and I never really considered it.

Way before hashtags.

Way before likes and followers.

Way before, any of us tried to brand peace and humility as if it were new.

Being low-key and hater-free is more than a catchphrase.

It's a **biblical blueprint.**

It's how Jesus walked.

It's how true wisdom flows.

It's how peace manifests in a loud, performance-driven, ego-driven world.

This isn't about playing small.

It's about knowing when to shine—and when to sit back and let your work speak for itself.

Let's break it down.

✓ **Stay Humble. Stay Grounded. Stay Low Key.**

We're living in an age where everyone wants to be seen, reposted, and celebrated. But the kingdom of God doesn't work like that. Not everything good needs a camera in front of it. Not every victory needs a caption.

"Let someone else praise you, and not your own mouth; an outsider, and not your own lips." — Proverbs 27:2

Jesus — the literal Son of God — stayed low-key.

He could've come through shining in gold, surrounded by armies, performing public miracles 24/7 to flex. But He didn't.

He rode into the city on a donkey.

He healed quietly.

He told people, *"Don't tell anyone I did this."*

He washed feet. He served.

Jesus wasn't chasing clout — He was walking in purpose.

"Make it your ambition to lead a quiet life: you should mind your own business and work with your hands..."
— 1 Thessalonians 4:11

And He wasn't the only one.

✓ **Moses** led millions out of slavery, but Scripture says he was *"more humble than anyone else on the face of the earth"* (Numbers 12:3)

✓ **Ruth** stayed faithful and steady — no bragging, no demands — and ended up part of the lineage of Jesus.

✓ **Mother Teresa** served the poorest of the poor in silence — not for fame, but because she believed they deserved dignity.

These were world changers.

And yet? They weren't loud about it.

So hear this:

- ✓ **There is a time and place to shine.**
- ✓ God will open doors and put you in rooms where you're meant to speak, lead, and be seen. Don't run from those moments. Step into them with grace.

- ✓ But boasting and bragging? That's not the way. And hating on others? That'll kill your peace and slow your purpose.

- ✓ **People will notice you.**
  They'll recommend you.
  They'll give awards and share your name in rooms you haven't entered — all *because* you did your work with heart and humility.
  I know. It happens to me and others all the time.

- ✓ Some of the most outstanding leaders in history didn't chase recognition.
  They chased impact.
  And in return? Recognition chased *them.*

2. Peace Over Pettiness — Always.

You can't live low-key if you're always getting pulled into nonsense. You can't be hater-free if you're constantly feeding off other people's negative energy.

> *"Do not repay anyone evil for evil… If it is possible, as far as it depends on you, live at peace with everyone."*
> — *Romans 12:17–18*

- ✓ **Jesus never wasted time on petty.**
  When they mocked Him, He stayed silent.
  When they tested Him, He answered with wisdom.
  When they crucified Him, He said, *"Father, forgive them."*

He *could've snapped.*

He *could've clapped back.*

But He knew... **real power doesn't always respond.**

"A gentle answer turns away wrath, but a harsh word stirs up anger."
— *Proverbs 15:1*

✓ **Your peace is your power.**
   And sometimes, the highest level of strength is simply **not reacting.**

✓ You don't need to match energy — you need to manage yours. You don't need to respond to every insult — you need to protect your purpose.

✓ Let them talk. Let them doubt. Let them scroll past.

Stay locked in. Stay elevated. Stay unbothered.

3. Haters Gonna Hate — You Just Don't Have to Be One.

Let's talk about it.

Not all hate comes from outside. Sometimes it creeps up inside of us quietly. We see someone winning, and it stings a little. We see someone getting credit, and we wonder, *"Why not me?"*

That's real — but it's not where we stay.

"Love your enemies and pray for those who persecute you."
— *Matthew 5:44*

Jesus never taught revenge. He taught *release.* He taught us to love differently. To live differently. To show grace even when it isn't shown to us.

And here's what's real:

You don't have to tear someone else down to rise. You don't have to compare. You don't have to compete.

You're in your **own** lane — your **own** assignment. What God has for you is **custom-built**. You don't need to rush it or resent somebody else's blessings.

You're not them. And they're not you. And that's precisely how it's supposed to be.

So clap for others. Cheer them on. Pray for them. **Do the opposite of what the world expects. That's Kingdom: living with the mindset and heart of God's Kingdom, doing things that reflect God's love.**

4. Keep Your Mind Right. That's Where Peace Begins.

This is the core of everything.

> *"You will keep in perfect peace those whose minds are steadfast because they trust in You." — Isaiah 26:3*

Your vibe, your focus, your mood, your reactions — they all start in your **mind.**

Peace isn't a place. It's not a playlist or a weekend off. **It's a posture.**

You've got to protect your thought life. Guard what you let in. Speak life over yourself. Root your identity in truth — not attention, not affirmation, not applause.

The more you trust God, the less you need validation from anybody else.

Final Word:

Low-key and Hate-Free isn't a weakness. It's *wisdom.* It's not hiding. It's *healing.* It's not being small. It's *being strategic.*

It's doing the work when nobody's clapping. It's staying grounded when others are chasing titles. It's letting your fruit talk and your faith walk.

Jesus walked low. Served low. Spoke truth. Moved with grace. And yet — **He changed everything.**

You don't need to push your name into every room. **Do the work. Keep your heart right. Let God do the rest.**

Because the spotlight?

It will find you when your light is real. The accolades? They'll come when your purpose is rooted. The world will see it — **but you don't have to show off to be seen.**

"God's been moving like this, low-key and hater-free. Now it's your turn."

FREQUENTLY ASKED QUESTIONS

Bonus Reflections on the Low-Key, Hater-Free Lifestyle

L et's be real—choosing to live low-key and hater-free in today's loud, hyper-connected world is a bold move. It goes against the grain of what we're taught: stay visible, stay relevant, stay chasing. So it's only natural that people have questions.

This lifestyle isn't just a vibe—it's a shift. And once you start moving different, thinking clearer, and protecting your peace, people are going to notice. This chapter answers some of the most common, real-life questions that come up when you commit to this path. These aren't just surface-level responses—this is guidance for anyone serious about staying grounded, avoiding drama, and thriving with quiet confidence.

1. Is being low-key the same as being antisocial or disconnected?

Not at all. Being low-key isn't about hiding from life—it's about choosing how you show up in it. You're not pulling away from people; you're just pulling away from unnecessary noise and drama. You can still be social, passionate, and present—but you're doing it on your terms. It's not disconnection—it's discernment. You're learning to pour your energy where it actually matters, not everywhere people expect.

Example: You might stop going to every party or happy hour, not because you're isolating, but because you're being selective about your energy. Instead of group chats or public updates, you connect more meaningfully one-on-one. That's not antisocial—that's intentional.

2. How do I stay low-key in a world obsessed with likes, views, and status?

It takes intention. You start by being more mindful of your energy. Every post, every comment, every response—ask yourself, "Am I doing this for me or for approval?" You don't have to disappear—you just have to stop performing. Let people wonder. Let them speculate. Meanwhile, you're moving in silence, building, healing, creating, growing. Quiet doesn't mean stagnant. It means sacred.

Example: Maybe you earned a new certification or started a new job. Instead of announcing it to the world right away, you quietly celebrate with your close friends or family. You still share the win—but on your terms, not for applause.

3. What if people think I'm acting distant or secretive when I stop oversharing?

Let them. The people who love you for who you are—not what you share—will stay close. The rest may fall off, and that's part of the process. Protecting your peace may confuse those who had unlimited access to your life before. But remember: you don't owe everyone visibility into your journey. The more you grow, the less explaining you'll want to do. And that's okay.

Example: You used to post daily updates, but now you keep your relationship, goals, and moves private. Some folks may assume you're "acting funny." But those who really know your heart will understand—and stay.

4. Can someone really live hater-free? Isn't that impossible?

Haters will always exist. That part's real. But living hater-free means you don't carry their energy in your heart or your head. You don't give their opinions a seat at your table. The goal isn't to eliminate hate— it's to elevate your mindset so high it can't touch you. You stop entertaining gossip. You stop reacting to every jab. You stay centered, grounded, and focused. That's what being hater-free is about.

Example: Someone makes a slick comment online or in person, trying to get a reaction. Instead of clapping back, you smile and keep it moving. You don't waste your time matching negative energy.

5. What if the hate is coming from people I care about—family, friends, coworkers?

That hits different. But even then, you have to protect your peace. Sometimes, the hardest boundaries are the ones we have to place with people we love. Being low-key and hater-free doesn't mean cutting everyone off—it means knowing who can sit in your inner circle and who needs to stay at the gate. Love people from a distance if you need to. Your mental health is not up for negotiation.

Example: A close friend starts throwing shade when you grow or evolve. Instead of engaging in drama, you give them space. You keep the connection respectful—but you no longer let them drain you.

6. Can I still be ambitious and successful while being low-key?

Without question. Low-key doesn't mean lazy or unmotivated—it means your success is built, not broadcasted. You're not posting every move; you're making moves. You're not talking about the plan; you're executing the plan. And when it all comes together, people will wonder how it happened—and that's the point. Let your silence build a future worth the wait. You don't need applause to accomplish.

Example: You're working on a big project, a side hustle, or going back to school. Nobody knows because you're focused on the work, not the announcement. Later, when it pays off, people will be shocked—but you won't. You knew what you were building the whole time.

7. What if I slip up and fall into comparison, gossip, or negativity again?

You're human—it happens. Sometimes, you'll catch yourself scrolling too long, comparing too much, or even feeling a little jealous of someone else's success. That doesn't make you a bad person; it makes you real. But here's the truth: hating on someone else won't speed up your blessings. Your time will come, but only if you focus on your path, not theirs. Let their win be proof that success is possible. Use it as fuel, not frustration. The key is to catch yourself, reset, and stay in your lane. You can't grow if you're always looking sideways.

Example: You see a peer taking trips, buying things, or making moves. For a second, you feel like you're behind. But then you catch it, breathe, and remind yourself, "My pace is my peace." You log off, refocus, and get back to your goals.

8. How can I inspire others to live this way without sounding preachy or "too deep"?

You don't have to say much; just be the example. People notice peace. They feel when you're moving differently. When they ask what's changed, you tell them straight: "I'm living a low-key, hater-free lifestyle." Say it with clarity and confidence. And if someone asks how you're doing? Look them in the eye and say, "Low-key and hater-free." Say it with conviction. Let that energy speak louder than any sermon ever could. When you live in it, you don't have to convince people they'll want the same peace for themselves.

Example: A coworker or friend says, "You seem different. Calmer." That's your moment to say, "I've just been keeping things low-key and hater-free." You're not trying to convert anybody. You're just living proof.

9. What if people don't respect my new mindset or boundaries?

Some people won't. Especially if they benefitted from the old version of you—the one who didn't have boundaries, who gave too much, who said yes too often. But boundaries are how you teach people how to treat you. At first, it might cause tension. But over time, the people who truly value you will adjust. And the ones who can't? They were never for you anyway. Your peace is too valuable to sacrifice for anyone's comfort.

Example: You used to answer every call, reply instantly, and be available 24/7. Now, you say "no" sometimes. You take time for yourself. And yeah, some people don't like the shift. That's fine. Peace is the priority now.

10. What's the biggest benefit of being low-key and hater-free?

Peace. Real, deep, unshakable peace. You stop living for applause and start living for alignment. You gain clarity, focus, and freedom. You protect your energy like the asset it is.

You're no longer driven by performance and let me be clear: that doesn't mean you stop giving your best. It doesn't mean you stop showing up, leveling up, or going hard in whatever you pursue. You should absolutely strive for excellence in everything you do. But the kind of "performance" we're leaving behind is the exhausting need to impress, prove, or post just to be seen. It's performing for approval instead of working from purpose.

You stop showing off and start showing up. You no longer move to be accepted—you move because you're aligned. You're no longer trying to fit in. You're focused on standing solid in who you are. When that clicks? You become unstoppable. Quiet confidence. Silent strength. That's the win. That's the lifestyle.

Example: You wake up in the morning not feeling the pressure to perform, post, or explain yourself. You go to bed at night with a clear mind, not thinking about how to impress or outdo anybody. That peace is priceless.

11. Can People in High-Profile or Demanding Roles Be Low-Key and Hater-Free?

Yes—absolutely. Living low-key and hater-free isn't about the job title or platform. It's about the mindset behind how you carry yourself, how you handle pressure, and how you choose peace in environments built for noise. It's not about invisibility—it's about intentionality. You can be visible without being loud. Influential without being flashy. Powerful without being performative. It's about knowing who you are and not needing the world to validate it for you.

You don't need to announce every move. You don't have to fight for attention to be effective. Sometimes, the real power shows up in how you don't react, how you protect your peace, and how you move in silence with purpose.

Here's how people in different roles can embody this lifestyle with clarity, strength, and grace:

✓ Politicians:

In the political world, the noise is constant—polls, press, debates, and opinions flying from every direction. But a **low-key, hater-free politician** moves with a different rhythm. They don't perform for likes or trend on social media—they serve the people who actually elected them. They're not chasing headlines—they're chasing long-term solutions. They don't spend their time clapping back or trying to win every debate—they speak when it matters, and they speak with intention.

Their power doesn't come from how loud they are—it comes from how clear and grounded they are. They're strategic, not reactive. They stay above petty politics and beneath-the-surface jabs because they're too focused on policies that create real change. When people criticize them (and they will), they don't spiral into defensiveness. They stay steady, rooted in service, and guided by values—not vibes.

They know: **you don't have to scream to lead. But if you speak, let it shake systems—not just stir up drama.**

They're proof that you can be visible without being flashy, bold without being belligerent, and powerful without being performative.

✓ Religious Leaders:

There's this quiet pressure in spiritual spaces to appear perfect—to have all the answers, the right words, the polished image. But the most impactful, **low-key, hater-free religious leaders** know better. They don't lead from a platform of pride—they lead from a posture of presence. They walk with people. They pray behind closed doors. They care more about *feeding souls* than gaining followers.

Charles E Tyler

They're not posting every sermon highlight or fishing for affirmation online. Their leadership shows up in how they comfort someone in crisis, how they teach with love, how they live the message—not just preach it. And when hate comes (because even spiritual leaders get hated on), they don't retaliate—they respond with grace. They don't argue theology on social media or try to prove their anointing. They let their peace, consistency, and humility speak for them.

They stay hater-free by staying focused on their *calling*, not their *clout*. They stay low-key by remembering the goal isn't fame—it's *faithfulness*.

And when they do speak up, it's not for ego—it's for edification.

✓ *Teachers:*

Teachers might not be trending, but they're transforming lives every single day. A **low-key, hater-free teacher** doesn't need applause, social media praise, or a "Teacher of the Year" plaque to know they're making a difference. They show up early, stay late, and pour into students in ways that rarely get noticed—but always get remembered. They bring snacks for the kid who forgot lunch, pull students aside when they see something's off, and stay after class to help one more time.

They're the reason a kid believes in themselves again. The reason a teen dares to dream bigger. They're not looking to go viral—they're planting seeds. Seeds of confidence, resilience, and hope. And long after the school year ends, their impact continues to grow in ways they may never even see.

And when the haters come? The ones who don't respect the profession, who question the "real value" of a teacher, who think they know better? They don't let it rattle them. They stay focused on the students, not the spectators. They don't fight for validation—they *teach through it*. That's how they stay low-key, grounded in the mission, and hater-free through the mess.

> *They're the real MVPs—the quiet kind. The kind who don't need a stage to change a life.*

✓ *Millionaires and Billionaires:*

The loudest room isn't always the richest one—and the richest ones aren't always the loudest. A **low-key, hater-free millionaire or billionaire** isn't interested in stunting for social media. They're not chasing viral flexes—they're building generational impact. While others post luxury, they're creating opportunity. Funding scholarships. Mentoring startups. Uplifting communities. And doing it all without shouting their good deeds.

Their success isn't built on ego—it's built on intention. They understand that true wealth isn't about what you can show—it's about what you can share. They live in peace because they're not performing. They don't need to prove anything to anybody. Their money moves in silence, but their impact echoes loudly.

And when haters assume they're stingy or disconnected? They don't feel the need to argue or explain. They don't post receipts—they keep doing the work. Their joy isn't tied to being seen—it's tied to being *useful*. They're not hiding; they're just *focused*. And that quiet focus? It's what makes their legacy last.

Because when you know what you've built, you don't need to broadcast it.

When your heart is generous and your mind is clear—there's no room for hate.

✓ *Influencers and Creatives:*

In a digital world that rewards noise, the ones who *last* are the ones who know how to stay grounded. A **low-key, hater-free creative** isn't in it for the constant applause—they're in it for the craft, the message, the meaning. They're not trying to post every single moment or ride every trend—they're creating from a real place. From experience. From emotion. From truth.

They're not chasing the algorithm—they're chasing *alignment*. They make content that feels like them, not what they think will go viral. They're okay with not posting for a while if it means protecting their peace. They take breaks when they need them, without a long explanation. They prioritize their mental health over their mentions, and they're not afraid to unplug in a world that's always plugged in.

And when haters come for their style, their pace, their voice? They don't argue—they don't explain—they don't adjust their lane for likes. They know not everyone will get it—and that's okay. They're not creating for everyone. They're creating for the ones who *feel it*. And their art? It speaks louder than any online presence ever could.

They stay low-key by moving with intention, not impulse. They stay hater-free by choosing *substance over spectacle*.

Because in a world full of noise, authenticity is the loudest thing you can offer.

And when you're rooted in who you are, you don't have to shout—you just *create and let it echo.*

Judges, County Executives, and Community Leaders:

A **low-key, hater-free judge** understands the weight of their decisions and doesn't use the bench to boost their ego or make a name for themselves. They listen deeply, consider context, and treat every person with dignity—because justice isn't about flexing power; it's about applying principles. They don't seek the spotlight, nor do they chase media moments. Instead of reacting to critics or defending every ruling, they stay rooted in the law and lead with quiet confidence. When backlash comes, they don't break character. They don't match the noise—they keep their focus. They know their legacy is built in the courtroom, not in the comments. That's power wrapped in poise.

A **low-key, hater-free county executive** knows that real leadership isn't about micromanaging or chasing political clout—it's about empowering others, trusting your team, and creating systems that actually serve people. They move with humility, ask more questions than they answer, and lead from a place of responsibility—not ego. When opposition or criticism shows up, they don't get flustered or distracted. They let the results speak. They don't waste time trying to silence every critic—they just keep doing the work. Calm, capable, and committed to progress over praise, they move through storms with steadiness and refuse to entertain unnecessary noise. That's how they stay effective *and* at peace.

And the **low-key, hater-free community leader**? They're the heartbeat of the neighborhood. They lead with presence, not performance. They don't need a title to have impact—they show up in real places, at real times, for real people. They're in the food drives, the PTA meetings, the tough conversations, and the quiet organizing sessions. And when critics question their motives or try to minimize their work, they don't fire back—they stay focused. They understand their role isn't to be popular; it's to be *purposeful*. They're not online defending themselves—they're in the streets defending their community. They don't need applause to know they're making a difference. Their actions speak, their consistency builds trust, and their humility keeps them grounded through it all.

✓ *Entrepreneurs and Business Owners:*

In hustle culture, the pressure to always be "on" is real. To constantly promote. Constantly produce. Constantly prove something. But a **low-key, hater-free entrepreneur** moves with a different energy. They're not chasing attention—they're chasing *alignment*. They don't need to post every win or flex every sale. They let the quality of their work—and the way they treat people—do all the talking.

They're not building their brand on hype—they're building it on trust. While others are trying to go viral, they're focused on creating something sustainable. Clients come back not because they saw a flashy ad—but because they felt something real. A genuine connection. Consistency. Value. They understand that branding isn't about shouting—it's about *showing up* the right way, again and again.

And when the critics come? When people question their quiet grind or downplay their progress? They don't get defensive. They don't get distracted. They *deflect the drama* and keep building. They're not here to argue—they're here to *deliver*. That's how they stay hater-free. They don't lead with ego. They lead with results.

They stay low-key because their peace is more important than popularity.
They stay hater-free because they're too focused on purpose to waste time proving anything.

Quiet excellence will always outlast loud mediocrity. And when your brand is built on substance, you don't need a spotlight—you become the standard.

✓ *Athletes and Coaches:*

Sports often come with ego, expectation, and pressure to perform—not just on the field, but in front of the cameras, the fans, and the media. But the truly great ones? The **low-key, hater-free athletes and coaches**—they move differently. They train in silence. They don't need to post every workout or talk trash before the game. They let their work speak. They show up for their *team*, not for attention.

Low-key athletes know when to lead and when to listen. They don't have to dominate the room—they dominate with discipline. They respect the game, stay coachable, and understand that greatness comes from what you do when no one's watching. Their humility *is* their edge. And when the wins come? They celebrate with grace. When the losses hit? They own it without excuses.

The best coaches set that same tone. They're not screaming for control or spotlight—they're building something deeper. They teach the game, yes—but more importantly, they teach *life*. They help shape men and women of character. They lift their players up, even when no one else sees the effort. They're steady through the ups and downs, focused on the growth—not just the glory.

And when hate comes—from critics, commentators, or even teammates—they don't feed into it. They don't clap back. They don't take the bait. They protect the locker room, protect their mindset, and keep their ego in check. That's how they stay **low-key** in the spotlight and **hater-free** in a competitive world.

They don't just play the game—they honor it.

They don't just coach the team—they elevate it.

And they lead with more than skill—they lead with substance.

✓ *Healthcare Professionals (Doctors, Nurses, Therapists):*

Every day, they hold lives in their hands—and they do it without seeking applause. A **low-key, hater-free healthcare worker** shows up when things are falling apart and brings calm into chaos. They're steady in crisis, composed under pressure, and compassionate without needing credit. Whether they're stitching a wound, holding a hand, or offering quiet support in a dark moment—they do it all from a place of service, not spotlight.

They absorb pain that isn't theirs. They take on the emotions, stress, and trauma of others—and still find a way to smile. They listen when people are scared. They care even when they're exhausted. They pour from a deep well of empathy, and they do it over and over again, not because they have to—but because they *want* to.

And when the outside world forgets how heavy that work is? When patients lash out or systems fail to appreciate them? They don't shut down. They don't lash back. They take a breath, refocus, and continue doing what they were called to do. That's how they stay hater-free— they know their impact isn't based on praise; it's based on people. The healing they give doesn't need to be broadcast—it's felt. Deeply. Quietly. Permanently.

They stay low-key because the work itself is sacred—it doesn't need to be performed.

They stay hater-free because their purpose is greater than public opinion.

They are the heartbeat of healing.

The calm in the storm.

The quiet heroes we never forget.

✓ *Law Enforcement and First Responders:*

There's a quiet courage in those who run *toward* danger instead of away. A **low-key, hater-free first responder**—whether they're law enforcement, a firefighter, an EMT, or a rescue worker—doesn't serve for status or recognition. They do it because it's wired into who they are. They're not trying to go viral or make headlines—they're trying to keep people safe and make it home with their integrity intact.

They show up with empathy, not ego. They de-escalate instead of dominate. They understand that real strength is shown in restraint, in reading the moment, and choosing peace when others might choose power. They protect communities, but they also build trust within them. They see people—not just situations. They listen. They act with care, especially when the world is watching—and *especially* when it isn't.

And when they're misunderstood, criticized, or hated for the badge or uniform they wear? They don't respond with pride or pettiness. They stay focused on the work. They lead with character. That's how they remain hater-free—by serving from the inside out, not for applause, but from a place of deep responsibility.

They stay low-key by doing the job with grace under pressure. They stay hater-free by remembering *why* they put that uniform on in the first place.

This is what real service looks like—silent, steady, and sincere.

✓ *Parents and Caregivers:*

This is the kind of love that rarely gets noticed—but it *literally* holds everything together. A **low-key, hater-free parent or caregiver** doesn't need the world to clap for them. They're in the trenches—changing diapers, managing chaos, cooking meals, giving rides, wiping tears, making sacrifices. Every day. Quietly.

They're not posting every milestone or seeking praise for the hard stuff—they're just doing it. Showing up. Holding it down. Building safe spaces for others to grow and feel loved. They carry the emotional weight of a household, often while managing their own struggles in silence. Caregivers give without asking for anything in return. Parents teach through actions more than words. Their love shows up in consistency, not performance.

And when the world overlooks them? When their work is taken for granted or their sacrifices are misunderstood? They don't explode. They don't seek validation. They just keep loving, keep showing up, and keep pouring into others. That's how they stay hater-free—by knowing their love has legacy, even if it's not always loud.

They stay low-key because their mission isn't to be seen—it's to support.

They stay hater-free because their purpose is rooted in care, not credit.

They are love in motion.

The glue in the background.

And the reason so many of us are still standing.

✓ *Managers and Supervisors:*

Middle management can feel like being caught between two waves—leadership above, team dynamics below. But a **low-key, hater-free manager** doesn't fold under pressure—they lead with calm and consistency. They don't manage for control—they guide with empathy. They don't treat people like numbers—they treat them like *humans*. They check in on their team's well-being, not just their to-do list. And when it's time to lead through challenges, they don't deflect blame or hog credit—they take responsibility and give praise where it's due.

Their leadership isn't loud—but it's *felt*. You can sense it in how the team communicates. How morale stays steady even when workloads grow. They build culture quietly, through trust and reliability, not flashy leadership slogans or performative pep talks.

And when they face resistance, gossip, or complaints behind closed doors? They don't retaliate. They don't micromanage out of fear. They stay rooted in clarity, compassion, and consistency. That's how they stay hater-free—by refusing to lead through ego or insecurity. They build respect the old-school way: through *showing up* and *following through*.

They stay low-key by not making it about them. They stay hater-free by keeping the focus on the team, the mission, and the bigger picture.

They make work feel human again—and that's leadership that lasts.

✓ *World Leaders:*

Yes—even at the global level, being **low-key and hater-free** isn't just possible—it's *powerful*. The best world leaders don't lead through fear or theatrics—they lead through clarity, calm, and conviction. They're not chasing the next headline or trying to make every speech go viral. They don't need to dominate the news cycle because they're focused on *making real decisions* that improve lives.

They know that unity is stronger than division. They stay composed in crisis. They listen to advisors. They weigh the consequences. And when they act, they do so with a sense of duty—not ego. Their strength isn't in volume—it's in vision. They don't need to constantly be seen to be respected. They move with wisdom, and they govern with grace.

And when the critics come—because world leaders are *always* criticized—they don't spiral into Twitter wars or seek validation through applause. They don't bend to popularity polls or swing with every public opinion. They stay grounded in values, mission, and long-term impact. That's how they stay hater-free. Not by being perfect—but by being *principled*.

They stay low-key because leadership isn't a performance—it's a responsibility.
They stay hater-free because their integrity is bigger than their image.

The world doesn't need louder leaders. It needs leaders who lead with quiet power and deep purpose.

✓ *College Presidents and Academic Leaders:*

In the world of higher education, where prestige, politics, and position can easily become traps, **low-key, hater-free academic leaders** move differently. They're not impressed by titles or corner offices—they're motivated by student success. They know the name on the building isn't more important than the student walking the hallway. They don't just lead from the boardroom—they walk the campus, listen to student voices, and pay attention to what's *really* happening on the ground.

They lead through listening, not just lecturing. They don't try to sound brilliant—they try to *be* present. They push for progress behind the scenes, advocating for access, inclusion, and innovation, but they don't need their name attached to every initiative. They know that true success isn't measured in speeches or ceremonies—it's in the kid who almost dropped out but finished strong because someone cared enough to intervene.

And when criticism comes—as it often does in academic spaces—they don't rush to defend their image or micromanage their teams to avoid bad press. They don't waste energy chasing prestige or responding to haters in faculty meetings or online. Instead, they stay focused on the mission: empowering minds, transforming lives, and shaping a better future through education.

They stay low-key by keeping their leadership student-centered, not self-centered.

They stay hater-free by choosing humility over hierarchy, and consistency over clout.

Because in the classroom of life, the best leaders don't just teach— they *reach*. And they don't just speak—they *serve*.

12. Can You Be Famous or a Household Name and Still Be Low-Key and Hater-Free?

Yes. You absolutely can. But it takes **intentionality**—how you live, what you share, and what you allow to get to you.

Being low-key isn't about whether people know your name—it's about how you manage your *energy*, your *access*, and your *peace*. Fame doesn't have to strip you of your privacy or authenticity. You can be known—but still selective. You can be successful—but still grounded. You can be seen—but not always accessible. It's not about disappearing—it's about *discerning*.

Here's how fame and low-key living can *coexist*:

✓ **They don't share everything.** Famous, low-key people control their narrative. They know what to post and what to protect. They don't let the media or social platforms define their story. They reveal what's purposeful—but keep what's sacred just that: *sacred*.

✓ **They don't chase the spotlight—the spotlight shows up where they already are.** Their presence isn't performative. They're not always posting, clapping back, or trying to stay "relevant." They focus on their *craft*, their *calling*, their *core*.

✓ • **They avoid drama.** Even when their name ends up in headlines, they don't let the noise dictate their moves. They don't respond to every rumor or feed every fire. They stay focused on the work, the mission, the *why*. That's hater-free living on a global level.

✓ Being famous doesn't mean you have to give all of yourself away. You don't have to overshare to stay relevant.

✓ You don't have to perform for people who don't understand your purpose.

✓ You can still *protect your peace* and walk in your assignment— without explaining yourself to the internet every day.

13. An additional question I was asked by a good friend:

Can You Still Be Low-Key and Hater-Free If You Love Luxury?

Absolutely. Loving luxury doesn't disqualify one from being low-key and hater-free. You can wear designer clothes, drive smooth cars, travel first class, and still maintain a humble demeanor. Having nice things doesn't mean you've sold out to vanity. It simply means you enjoy quality and comfort, and that's perfectly fine.

Being low-key isn't about rejecting success; it's about not performing with it. It's about not using what you have to prove who you are. You can live in abundance without needing to announce it. You can enjoy luxury without needing to flex it for likes or validation.

And being hater-free? That just means you're not letting envy, ego, or opinions run your life. You're not judging others for what they have and not adjusting your life to avoid being judged, either. You're grounded enough to enjoy what you've earned without making it anyone else's business.

So yes, you can have the Rolex, the tailored suits, the red bottoms, the fine wine, the elite experiences. Just don't need them to feel whole. Don't chase them for applause. Let them reflect your taste, not your identity.

Because when your spirit is solid, the shine is just a bonus.

Luxury isn't the problem. Performance is.

And peace? That's still the real flex.

You can be low-key, hater-free, and still love the finer things.

It's not about hiding success. It's about not letting it define you.

14. What's the bottom line?

Anyone—no matter their position, platform, or level of fame—can live low-key and hater-free. Whether you're running a classroom, a company, a courtroom, or a country—this lifestyle is available if you *choose it*. It doesn't shrink your reach—it *sharpens your impact*. It doesn't make you less relevant. It makes you *more rooted*.

You don't have to be loud to lead—but if you do raise your voice, let it be with *purpose*, like Dr. King. You don't have to fight every battle to win. You don't have to be seen to be solid.

Peace is the flex. Purpose is the posture. Low-key and hater-free isn't just possible—it's powerful.

FINAL MESSAGE:

LET'S TALK FOR A MINUTE

I f you've made it to this point, let me just say thank you. Seriously. This isn't one of those feel-good books you flip through and forget. This is a shift and a real one. And if something in these pages made you pause, nod, underline, or even just sit with the truth of it, then you're already changing. You're already doing the work.

Here's the thing: this lifestyle isn't about being perfect. It's about being real. It's about waking up and choosing peace over performance, growth over gossip, and alignment over applause. You don't need to have it all figured out. You don't have to disappear off the grid or explain your every move. But what you do need to do is protect your energy. Guard your peace. And remind yourself that a quiet life can still be a powerful one.

So what's next? Maybe you unfollow a few folks. Maybe you post less and pray more. Maybe you stop feeling like you owe anyone a play-by-play of your progress. Or maybe you just breathe a little easier, knowing not every win needs a witness to be real.

And if you slip up? Cool. Reset. Keep going. If people don't get it, let them talk. Your peace will speak louder than their opinions every time. If it gets lonely, you're not alone. There are plenty of us choosing quiet, choosing calm, choosing freedom—every day.

Now, let's be real, some people don't get the luxury of staying low-key. Throughout history, there have been leaders, truth-tellers, and changemakers who had to step up and speak out. Not because they wanted the spotlight but because purpose demanded it. And when they did, they shifted culture, saved lives, and changed the world for the better. Moving with purpose doesn't always mean staying in the background. Sometimes, the right thing to do is to rise, to speak, and to stand tall—on purpose.

The low-key lifestyle isn't for everyone... but the principles behind it can benefit anyone.

Not everyone wants to live quietly. Some people thrive in the spotlight. Some love the crowd, the energy, the constant connection. And that's okay.

But here's the thing—even the loudest lives need quiet moments. Even the boldest voices need rest.

Even the most visible people benefit from boundaries.

So, while being low-key in the literal sense (staying private, moving in silence, keeping your circle small) might not fit everyone's personality or season of life, the values behind it, like peace, purpose, authenticity, discernment, and emotional intelligence, absolutely apply across the board.

Whether you're a CEO, a student, a performer, a parent, or a public figure, learning how to protect your energy, move with intention, and rise above noise and negativity is powerful. And it transforms how you lead, love, build, and live.

So no—it's not for everyone. But yes—it has something for everyone. And that might be the most beautiful part of all.

Again, this lifestyle isn't for everybody. But if it's for you, lean into it. Grow in it. Rest in it. Walk it out. Just remember, being low-key doesn't mean you're hiding. Hater-free doesn't mean they'll stop hating. It just means you're no longer available for the noise.

This isn't about staying silent when it matters. It's about choosing peace and purpose over performance. Quiet isn't passive. Quiet is intentional.

Moving low-key doesn't mean moving passively. It means moving with purpose, not for performance.

So, keep going. Stay grounded. Stay solid. Stay blessed. Stay free.

Low-key and hater-free, for life! – Charles E Tyler